Paper Dolls

FASHION WORKSHOP

NORMA J. BURNELL

Quarto is the authority on a wide range of topics.
Quarto educates, entertains, and enriches the lives of our readers—
enthusiasts and lovers of hands-on living.
www.quartoknows.com

Artwork © 2016 Norma J. Burnell
Patterns and incidental doodles © Shutterstock.com

Acquiring & Project Editor: Stephanie Carbajal

Cover Design & Page Layout: Jacqui Caulton

6 Orchard Road, Suite 100
Lake Forest, CA 92630
quartoknows.com
Visit our blogs at quartoknows.com

Printed in China
3 5 7 9 10 8 6 4 2

Paper Dolls
FASHION WORKSHOP

NORMA J. BURNELL

Contents

CHAPTER 1
Getting Started

Tools & Materials

The tools and materials on these pages will help you create all of the fabulous fashions in this book.

Sketchpad and Drawing Paper Sketchpads come in many sizes and are great for working out your ideas.

Vellum Drawing Paper Vellum is a heavyweight, smooth-finish card stock that takes in color beautifully. It's perfect for finished drawings.

Tracing Paper Tracing paper is useful for tracing figures and creating a clean version of a sketch using a light box. (See "How to Use a Light Box," page 9.) Use quality tracing paper that is sturdy enough to handle erasing and coloring.

Pencils Graphite drawing pencils are designated by hardness and softness. H pencils are hard and make lighter marks; B pencils are soft and make darker marks. Pencils range from very soft (9B) to very hard (9H). Mechanical pencils are great for line quality and consistency of sharpness.

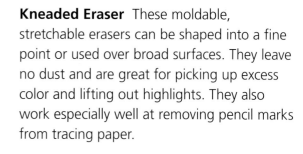

Kneaded Eraser These moldable, stretchable erasers can be shaped into a fine point or used over broad surfaces. They leave no dust and are great for picking up excess color and lifting out highlights. They also work especially well at removing pencil marks from tracing paper.

White Plastic/Vinyl Eraser Plastic or vinyl erasers are a staple in fashion drawing. They remove graphite without chewing up the paper and are best for erasing hard pencil marks and large areas.

Art Markers Professional art markers create bold, vibrant bands of color. They are great for laying down large areas of even color, as well as for shading.

Colored Pencils Colored pencils are a convenient and easy method for applying color. Professional-grade colored pencils have a waxy, soft lead that is excellent for shading and building up layers of color gradually.

Gel Pens Gel pens consist of pigment suspended in a water-based gel. They deliver thick, opaque color and work easily on dark or previously colored surfaces. They are perfect for finishing details in your illustrations or for adding sparkles, stitching detail, and accents.

Pigment-Ink Pens Technical pens are great for adding teeny, crisp details without bleeding.

How to Use a Light Box

A light box is a useful and generally inexpensive tool (although there are fancier, professional-grade versions). As its name suggests, a light box is a compact box with a transparent top and light inside. The light illuminates papers placed on top, allowing dark lines to show through for easy tracing. Simply tape your rough drawing on the surface of the light box. Place a clean sheet of paper over your original sketch and turn the box on. The light illuminates the drawing underneath and will help you accurately trace the lines onto the new sheet of paper. You can also create a similar effect by placing a lamp under a glass table or taping your sketch and drawing paper to a clear glass window and using natural light.

Basic Figure Proportions

The first step to drawing great paper doll models is to understand basic figure proportions. Below I've broken down the body into eight even sections represented by nine lines, so you can see where and how the various parts of the body relate to one other.

The head makes up one section, the body makes up three sections, the top half of the legs makes up two sections, and the bottom half of the legs and feet makes up two sections.

The palms of the hands generally fall at the top of the inner leg, and the elbows typically fall at the waist.

Remember that this is a general guide. Paper dolls, just like people, come in all shapes and sizes, so feel free to adjust for your creative frame of mind.

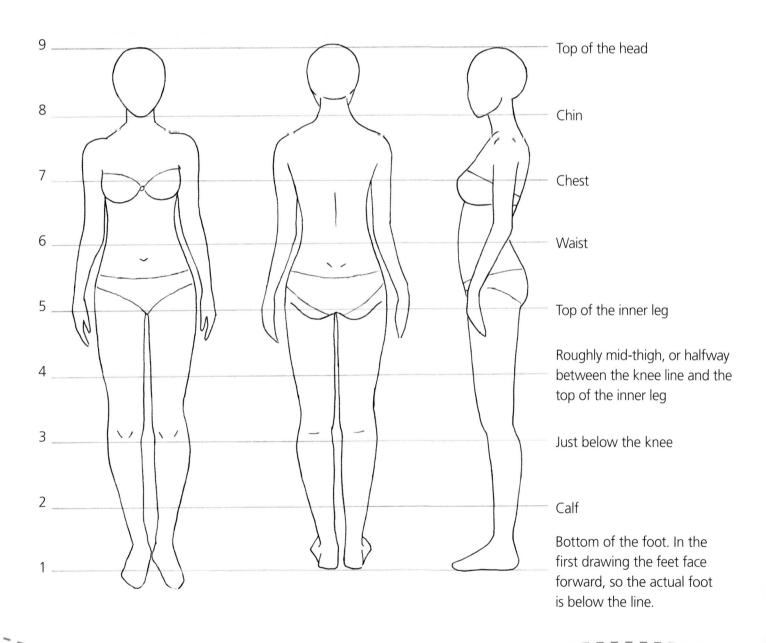

9 ———— Top of the head

8 ———— Chin

7 ———— Chest

6 ———— Waist

5 ———— Top of the inner leg

Roughly mid-thigh, or halfway between the knee line and the top of the inner leg

4

3 ———— Just below the knee

2 ———— Calf

Bottom of the foot. In the first drawing the feet face forward, so the actual foot is below the line.

1

Poses

The best poses for paper dolls are those that allow for good tab placement on the clothing. The poses on these pages are just a few examples of great paper doll poses. Use these to get started, but don't be afraid to try out your own fierce poses!

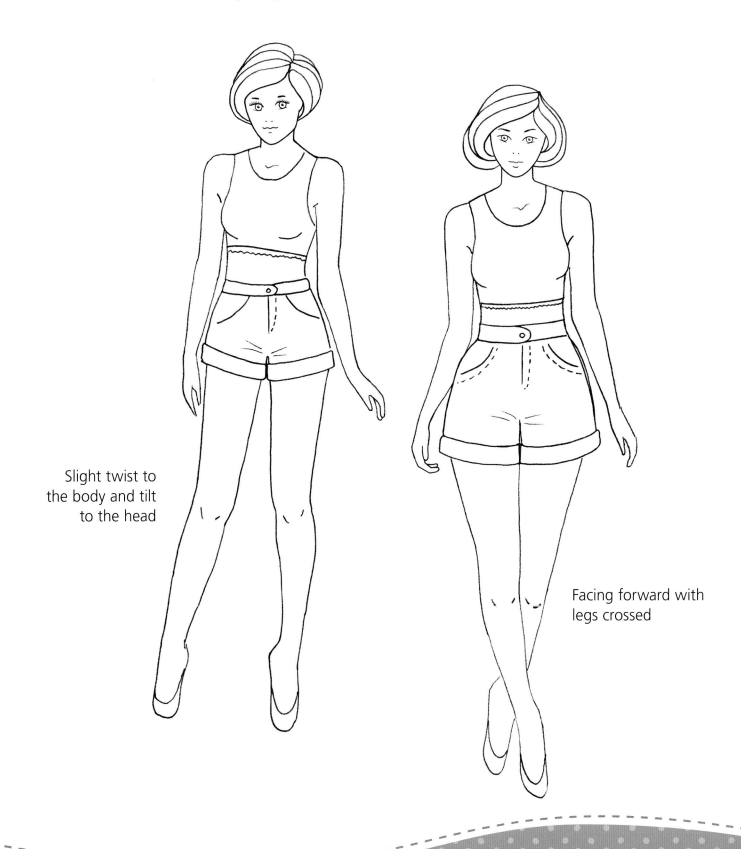

Slight twist to the body and tilt to the head

Facing forward with legs crossed

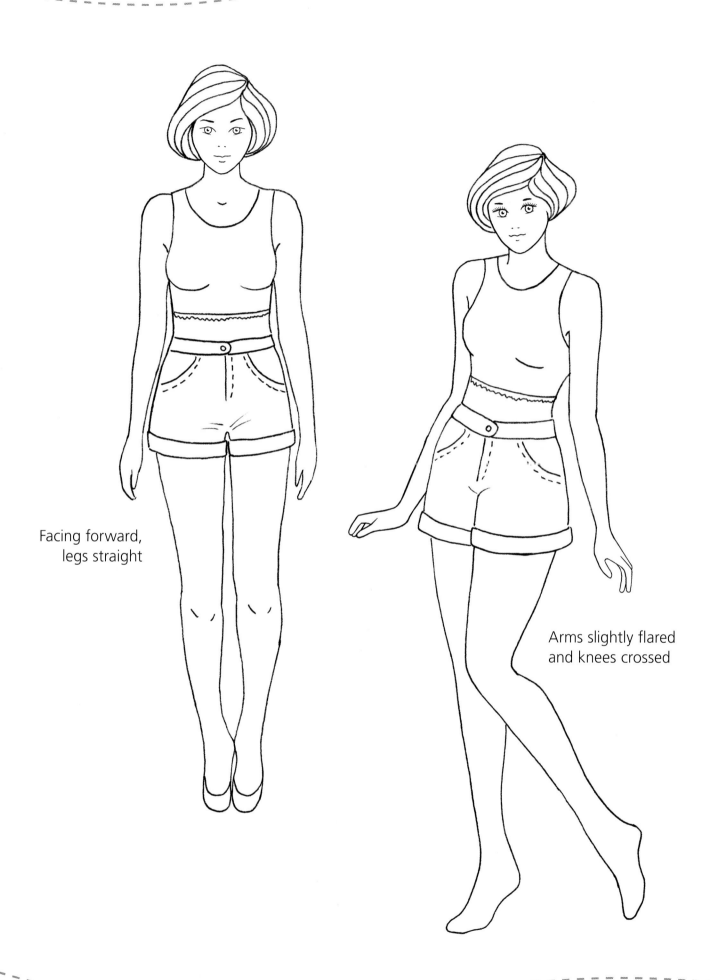

Facing forward,
legs straight

Arms slightly flared
and knees crossed

Fashion Drawing

Inspiration for creating paper dolls can come from many sources. Start paying closer attention to the fashions you see on the streets, in line at the coffee shop, at the beach, on TV shows, and even the grocery store—fashion and fabric is everywhere! Start by looking in your own closet...I did!

Gesture Drawing

Gesture drawings have long been used in figure study. These quick, rough drawings are designed to get the basic figure pose on paper as quickly as possible. They are a great way to practice proportions and loosen up. Gesture drawings are usually created on inexpensive paper with soft leads or charcoal, but you can use any medium you like. The idea is to practice and start sketching without worrying about the end result. The more you sketch and practice, the more your personal style will come through and the more comfortable you'll become with drawing the figure.

Fashion Sketches

Creating quick, colorful sketches of your doll wearing outfits is another great way to help you plan your fashions. Try various color combinations, and mix and match items of clothing.

Photocopy your undressed doll, and then draw outfits right over the copy. This way you can try out various designs and colors without having to re-draw the doll over and over! Once you have an outfit you like, you can make it more detailed and paper-doll ready with tabs and clean lines.

Playing with Color

Playing with color is one of the best parts of fashion design! To create shading effects, work with colors in the same color family (see below).

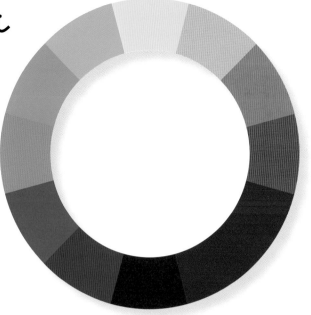

Pick out three colors in the same family—light, medium, and dark—and place them side by side. Overlap the colors and see what happens! Some colors blend together better than others. The best way to figure it out is to practice and see what works best.

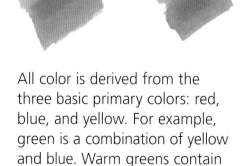

Complementary colors are opposite colors which, when combined, cancel each other out. They also create visual tension when next to each other.

All color is derived from the three basic primary colors: red, blue, and yellow. For example, green is a combination of yellow and blue. Warm greens contain more yellow, while cool greens have more blue.

Making Paper Dolls

Follow these steps to create a paper doll model. You can create as many dolls as you like, in a variety of poses and with a diverse range of features! Use the tips and suggestions on pages 11–12 to create good poses that will work well for paper doll clothing.

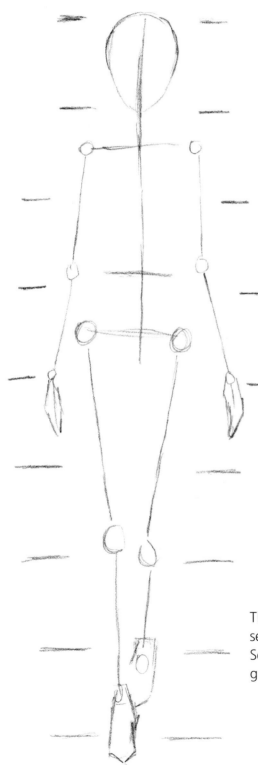

First draw a stick figure showing the basic proportions and pose. Draw horizontal lines to represent the shoulders, waist, and hips, and draw an oval for the head. Referencing the guidelines, determine the hand and foot placement. Once the placement for the head, hands, and feet is determined, the rest simply fits within this structure. Draw circles where the major joints are located: shoulders, elbows, hips, knees, wrists, and ankles.

The guidelines here help set up the right proportions. See page 10 for more tips on guidelines and proportions.

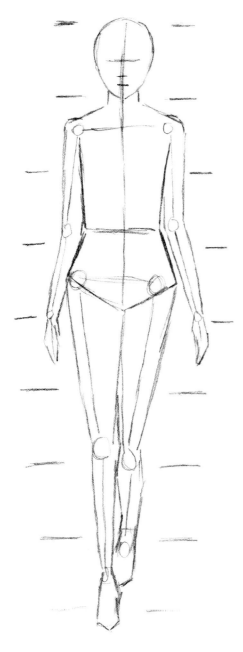

◄ Break down the body into basic shapes. Draw diagonal lines connecting the waist to the shoulders and hips. Sketch in some volume to the arms and legs, and work on defining the hands and feet.

► Next add curves and details. Follow your sketch to add curves to the chest, hips, arms, and legs. Sketch in horizontal lines for facial feature placement, and add some hair.

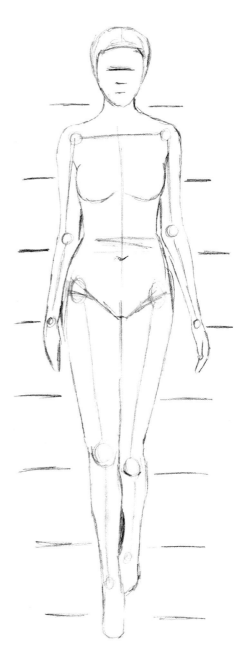

Artist's Tip

The circles represent major joints in the body. These are usually wider areas with muscles attached to them, so look to add curves and tension in these areas.

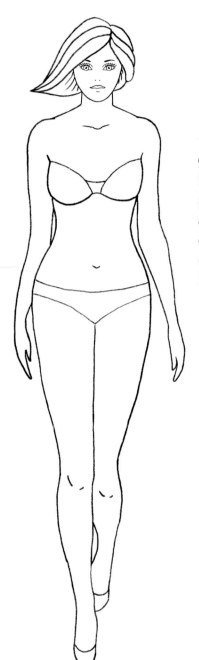

◄ Once the sketch is well-defined, carefully draw over the lines with a fine- or medium-point marker pen. I like to use a medium tip for the body outline and a fine tip for the details, such as the face and lace on the undergarments.

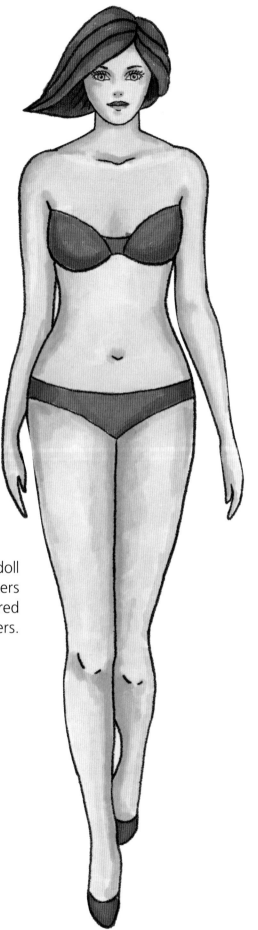

► Finish by coloring the doll with your favorite markers or colored pencils. I colored mine with markers.

Artist's Tip

Keep your lines clean and sharp, and use a slightly thicker pen so the doll will be easy to cut out.

Tab Placement

Tab placement is particularly important in order for your dolls' outfits to fit and stay in place. The following illustrations demonstrate general tab placement for basic poses. Keep in mind that the tab placement may need to be adjusted, depending on the doll's pose and the shape and complexity of the clothing.

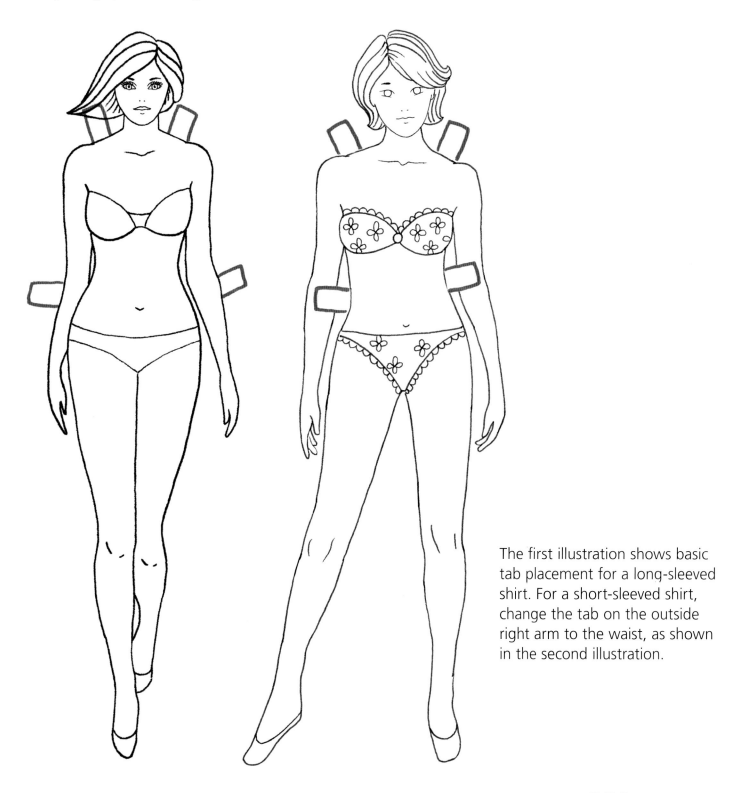

The first illustration shows basic tab placement for a long-sleeved shirt. For a short-sleeved shirt, change the tab on the outside right arm to the waist, as shown in the second illustration.

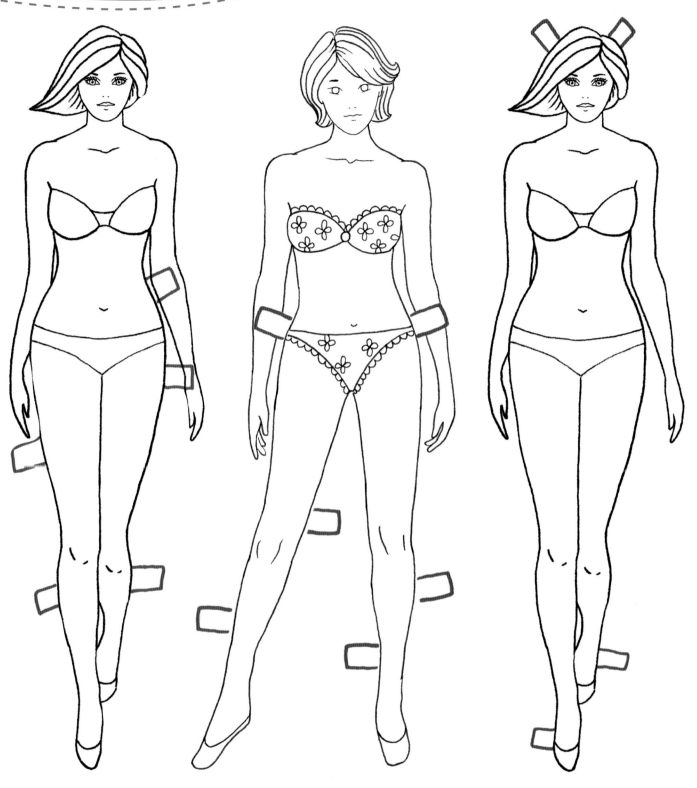

Tab placement for long pants with legs together

Tab placement for long pants with legs apart

This illustration shows the typical placement for hats or wigs and shoes. Keep in mind that shoes need smaller tabs. Also, if you design a large hat or updo hairstyle, you may need to increase the size of the tabs.

Fabrics & Prints

Fabrics come in all sorts of colors, prints, and textures. Different colors and patterns can give the same outfit or piece of clothing an entirely different look. Experiment with different mediums and techniques to achieve unique and creative designs—the sky is the limit!

On the same dress I've used three different patterns or prints.

◄ Here I applied random patches of blue, yellow, and orange for a loose and colorful effect. Note where the yellow and blue overlap, making green.

Artist's Tip

Experiment with overlapping colors and see what magic happens. It's also helpful to refer to a color wheel. (See page 15.)

Use squares and triangles in various sizes and color combinations for multiple effects.

Paisley patterns can be simple or complex.

Flower come in all shapes and sizes, and fabrics don't have to maintain perfectly even patterns. Many fabrics are made with custom or hand-painted patterns or silkscreen images.

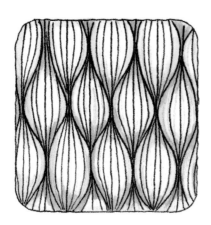

Line and shading greatly add to the flow of fabric.

Stacking oval shapes in a line is a simple way to create the look of knitted fabric.

Triangles make wonderful patterns. Try putting a triangle inside of another triangle, centered or off-centered for a varied effect.

Tangled Patterns

Tangled patterns, by their nature of repetition, make wonderful prints and textures for fabric. There are thousands of tangles to choose from and experiment with. Here are a few examples to help get you started!

  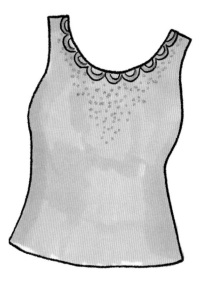

Try embellishing your outfits with appliqué shapes and patterns. Here I used a pattern of swirling squares to add fun sparkle and texture.

Use white or colored gel pens to add patterns to your outfits. Here I applied a simple paisley print with a white gel pen.

Add trim and sparkle. Here I added scalloped trim to the neckline and used a clear glitter pen to add a bit of sparkle to the top.

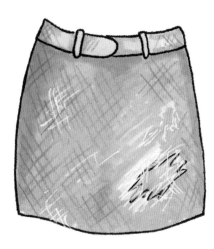 

To achieve a warm denim look, use several layers of blues for a base, and then crosshatch over the base colors with a sharp colored pencil. For stressed denim, let some skin show through a couple of holes, and roughly crosshatch with white gel pen around the edges of the holes.

To achieve a plaid effect, lay down a base color using the lightest color that will be in the fabric. Next, with a medium color, add striped lines in two directions. Repeat with the darkest color. For extra thin lines use colored pencil.

To create polka dots, you can lightly sketch them in pencil first and then color around them, or you can add them with a gel pen or paint after coloring. Try using various sizes and spacing for different effects.

Stripes can be horizontal, vertical, or diagonal. They can be thin or wide. Plan your stripes by drawing them with pen, or lightly in pencil for a more subtle stripe, as I have done here.

Stippling is a drawing technique that involves using small dots to render shading and texture. Here I used the technique to create a mottled look in the fabric.

Artist's Tip

For short-sleeved shirts, tabs must be placed at the waist.

CHAPTER 2
Apparel Basics

Casual Style

Whether she's out running errands, catching a movie with friends, or studying at the local coffee shop, this casual girl has serious style.

1

Start with a stick figure showing the basic proportions and pose. This doll has a slight tilt to her head and body, so I used a slight curve for the center line.

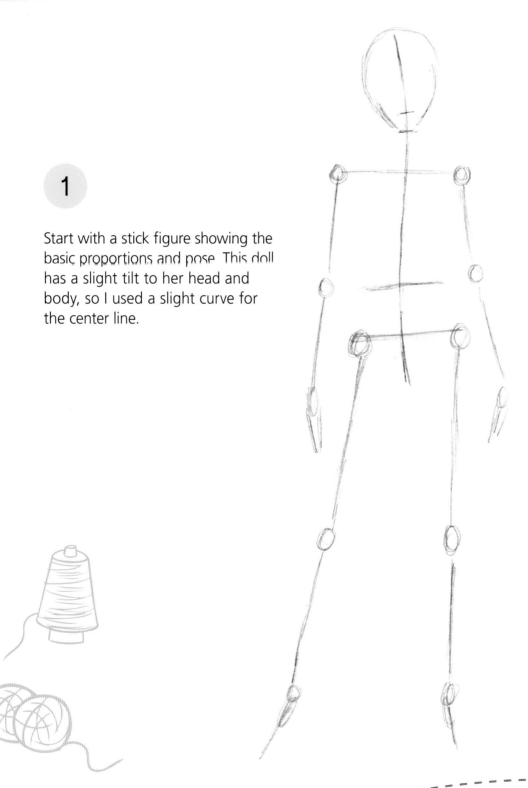

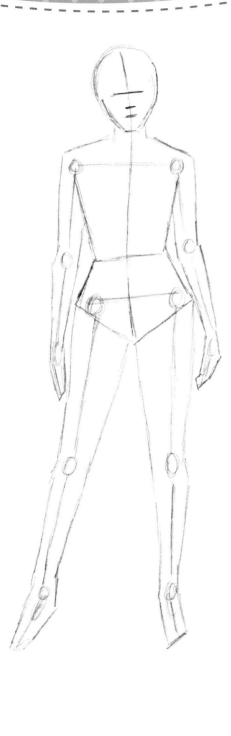

Next break down the body into basic shapes. Draw diagonal lines connecting the waist to the shoulders and hips. Sketch in some volume to the arms and legs, and work on hand and feet placement.

3

Add curves and details by following your sketch along the chest, hips, arms, and legs. Sketch in horizontal lines for the facial feature placement, and add some hair.

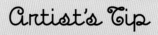

Artist's Tip

Keeping your dolls' hair on the shorter side makes tab placement easier. You can always create a wig or two for your doll!

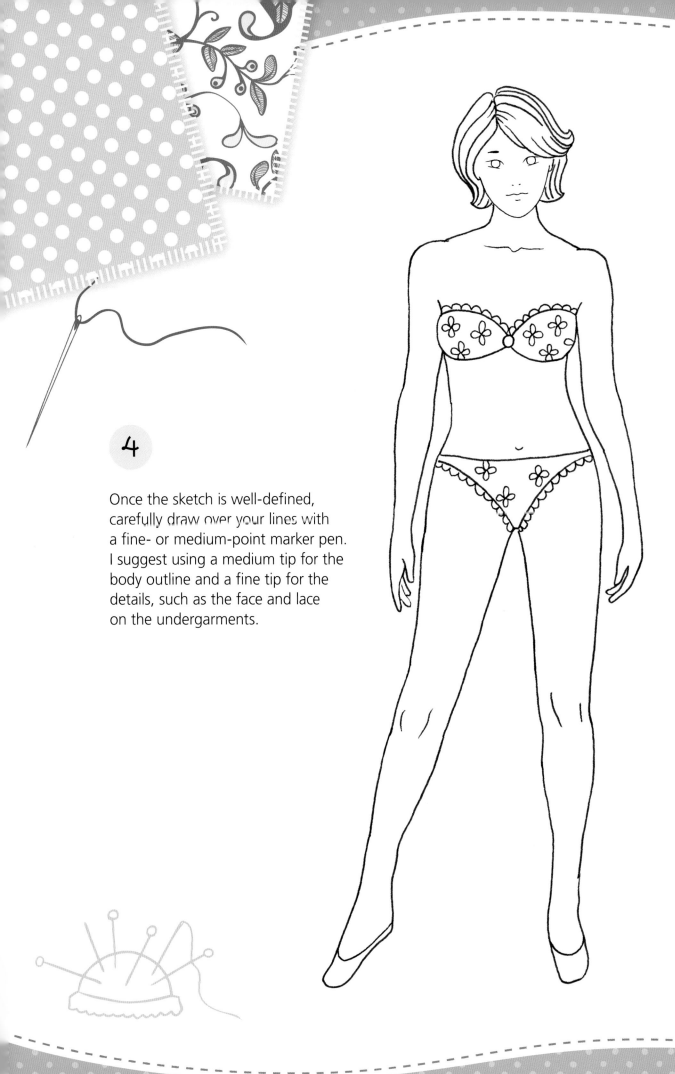

4

Once the sketch is well-defined, carefully draw over your lines with a fine- or medium-point marker pen. I suggest using a medium tip for the body outline and a fine tip for the details, such as the face and lace on the undergarments.

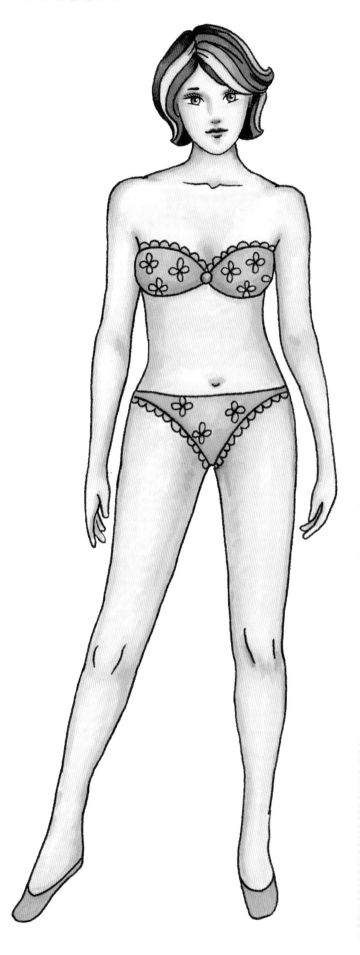

5

Color your doll using your favorite markers or colored pencils. For touches of realistic shading, start with the lightest colors first for a base of color. Then add darker shades in shadowed areas, such as under the chin and nose and inside the arms and legs.

Artist's Tip

I used extra-sharp colored pencils for the lips and eyes to achieve fine detail.

Skinny Jeans & Tee

Jeans are a must-have for any casual-chic outfit. Pair them with a flirty top, and you've got the makings for the perfect weekend look!

1

Sketch the outfit to fit over the doll by tracing around the doll's outline, following the lines and curves. Skinny jeans are one of the easiest articles of clothing to make, because they follow the outline of the body so closely.

Ruffles give this basic tee a flirty and feminine vibe.

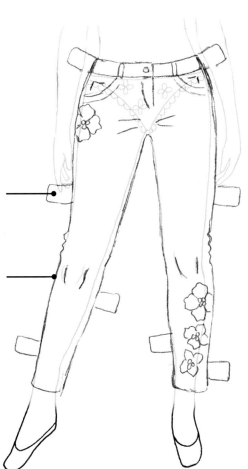

Pay attention to how the tabs will fit around the doll. Place them where they will fold and stay on the doll easily.

A few puckers at the knees adds a bit of realism, while contour lines shows the tightness of the fabric.

Artist's Tip

Sketch your outfits with light pencil strokes to make it easier to erase the pencil once you've outlined in marker.

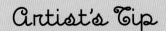

2

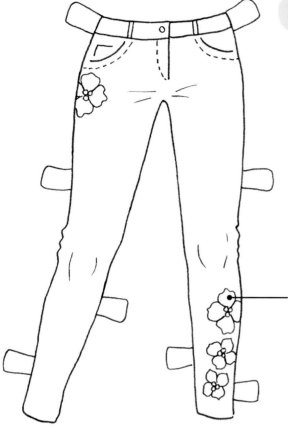

Once your sketch is finalized, trace over the lines with a fine- or medium-point marker pen. Erase any pencils lines, but be sure to let the pen dry before erasing to avoid smudging.

Add details, such as topstitching and floral patches.

Add details, such as a collar.

Define the ruffles.

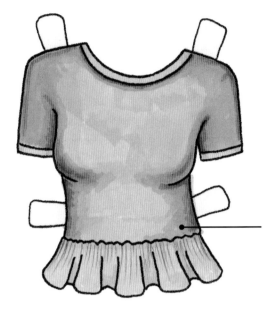

3

Add color with your favorite markers or colored pencils.

I used two shades of pink and started with the lighter color to lay down a base over the whole piece. Then I used a darker shade of pink to add shading and curves.

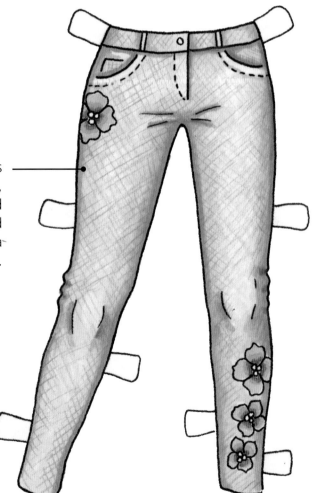

Here I used three shades of blue—light, medium, and dark. Then I used a very sharp colored pencil to crosshatch for a textured denim look.

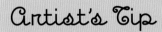

Artist's Tip

Start with the lightest shade to fill in an area, and then use medium and darker colors to add curves and shading.

Art Markers Professional art markers create bold, vibrant bands of color. They are great for laying down large areas of even color, as well as for shading.

Colored Pencils Colored pencils are a convenient and easy method for applying color. Professional-grade colored pencils have a waxy, soft lead that is excellent for shading and building up layers of color gradually.

Gel Pens Gel pens consist of pigment suspended in a water-based gel. They deliver thick, opaque color and work easily on dark or previously colored surfaces. They are perfect for finishing details in your illustrations or for adding sparkles, stitching detail, and accents.

Pigment-Ink Pens Technical pens are great for adding teeny, crisp details without bleeding.

How to Use a Light Box

A light box is a useful and generally inexpensive tool (although there are fancier, professional-grade versions). As its name suggests, a light box is a compact box with a transparent top and light inside. The light illuminates papers placed on top, allowing dark lines to show through for easy tracing. Simply tape your rough drawing on the surface of the light box. Place a clean sheet of paper over your original sketch and turn the box on. The light illuminates the drawing underneath and will help you accurately trace the lines onto the new sheet of paper. You can also create a similar effect by placing a lamp under a glass table or taping your sketch and drawing paper to a clear glass window and using natural light.

Basic Figure Proportions

The first step to drawing great paper doll models is to understand basic figure proportions. Below I've broken down the body into eight even sections represented by nine lines, so you can see where and how the various parts of the body relate to one other.

The head makes up one section, the body makes up three sections, the top half of the legs makes up two sections, and the bottom half of the legs and feet makes up two sections.

The palms of the hands generally fall at the top of the inner leg, and the elbows typically fall at the waist.

Remember that this is a general guide. Paper dolls, just like people, come in all shapes and sizes, so feel free to adjust for your creative frame of mind.

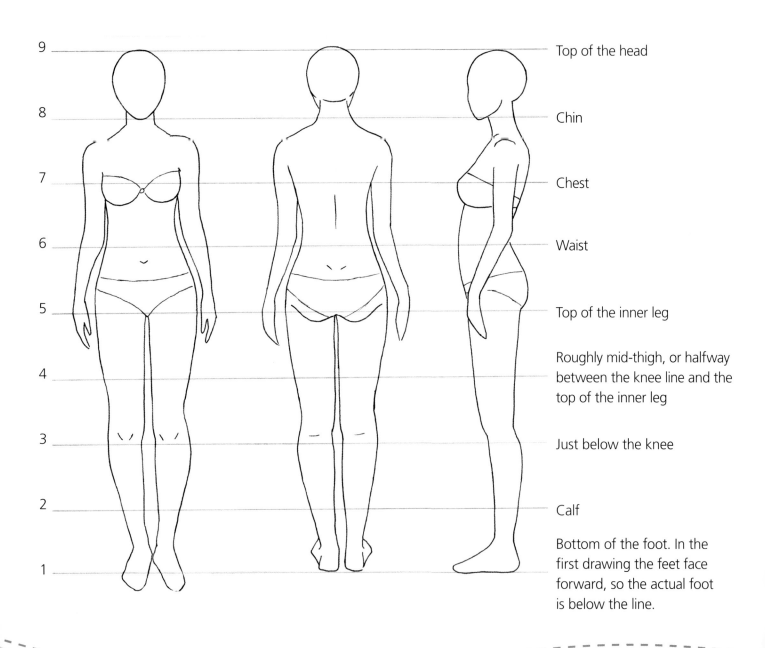

9 — Top of the head

8 — Chin

7 — Chest

6 — Waist

5 — Top of the inner leg

4 — Roughly mid-thigh, or halfway between the knee line and the top of the inner leg

3 — Just below the knee

2 — Calf

1 — Bottom of the foot. In the first drawing the feet face forward, so the actual foot is below the line.

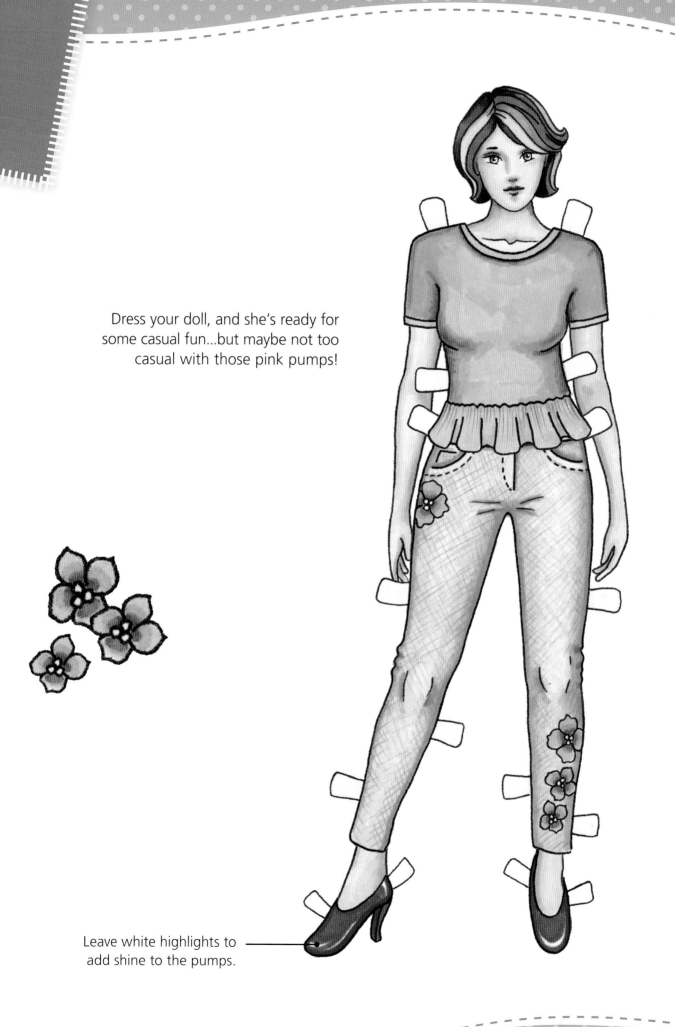

Dress your doll, and she's ready for some casual fun...but maybe not too casual with those pink pumps!

Leave white highlights to add shine to the pumps.

More Casual Tops

Buttons, pockets, and an appliqué design add pizzazz to this cardigan.

Soft pinks and lime green make this sweater perfect for a spring walk.

A sweater like this should be roomy. Add simple cables and pen marks for texture.

Perfect for an autumn afternoon!

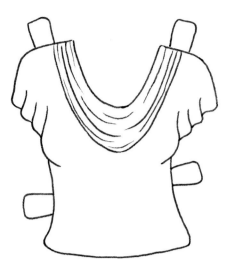

A swoop neck with a flowing collar and loose, folded sleeves gives this top dressy detail.

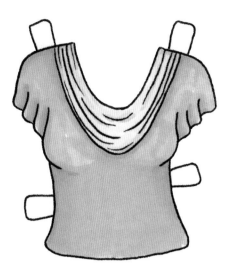

This shirt can be paired with jeans, shorts, a cute skirt...or just about anything!

Add some trim to the top and button-down opening.

Trace this tank closely to the doll's figure for a tight fit.

Lay down a solid color over the entire tank, and then add stripes. I used diagonal stripes on the top half and horizontal stripes on the bottom half.

Artist's Tip

Use a ruler to draw your stripes!

Other Casual Bottoms

The wide waistband and flared legs give these fun, patterned pants a 70s vibe.

I used two shades of green to create shading and curves. A thin line of shading down the line on each leg gives the pants a paneled look.

A simple A-line skirt is a necessity for any fashionista's wardrobe.

Add polka dots or stripes for a fun pattern.

You can never have too many pairs of colorful shorts. I made a green and pink pair for easy mixing and matching.

Don't forget footwear!

Sleepwear

There's nothing like curling up with a good book when you're wrapped up in your favorite soft, fuzzy robe!

Start with a lighter color to add a layer of color over the whole robe, and then add shading with a darker color in the folds and creases.

Create terry-cloth texture using colored pencils to add little circles and squiggles all over the fabric.

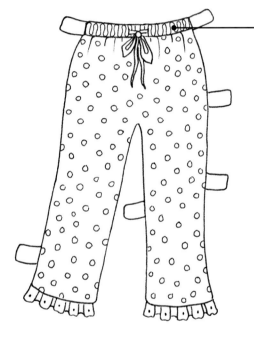

Use simple squiggles to indicate an elastic waistband.

Add a polka-dot or heart pattern, and color with markers or colored pencils.

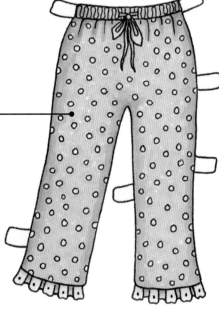

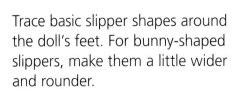

Trace basic slipper shapes around the doll's feet. For bunny-shaped slippers, make them a little wider and rounder.

You could also try making panda bear, kitty, or puppy slippers!

CHAPTER 3
Getting Dressy

All Dressed Up

Every girl needs a bevy of beautiful dresses and other fancy outfits suitable for a night out on the town, party, dance, or other special event.

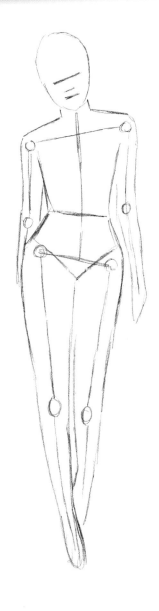

Draw a stick figure showing the basic proportions and pose. Draw horizontal lines to represent the shoulders, waist, and hips. Draw circles for the head and major joints: shoulders, elbows, hips, knees, wrists, and ankles. Break down the body into basic shapes. Connect the waist to the shoulders and hips. Sketch in volume in the arms and legs, and refine the hand and feet placement.

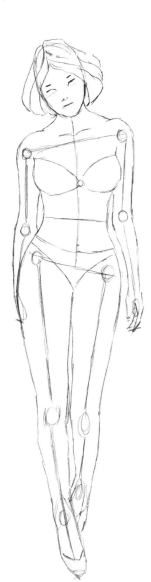

Next add curves and details. Following your sketch, add curves to the chest, hips, arms, and legs. Sketch in horizontal lines for the facial feature placement, and add some hair.

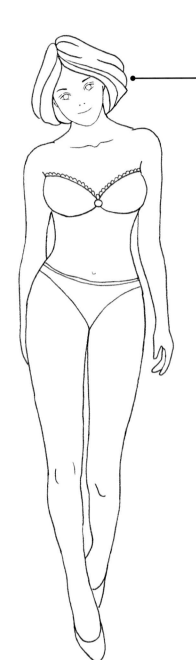

I left my face very simple because I want to add detail

3

Once the sketch is well-defined, carefully draw over the lines with a fine- or medium-point marker pen.

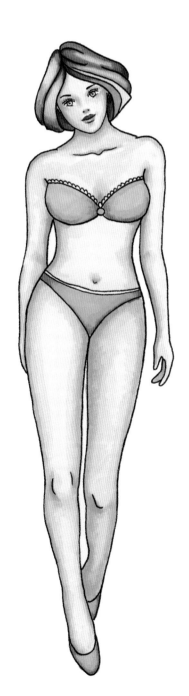

4

Use your favorite markers or colored pencils to finish the doll. I gave mine a pink bra and panties with a little lace trim.

Cocktail Dresses

To achieve the spaghetti-strap look and still have tabs to hold the dress in place, trace very closely to the doll's outline along the shoulders—you'll color this part with skin tones.

Every girl needs a classic black dress. This dress is formfitting, so trace closely to the doll's figure. Little pucker lines at the waist add a touch of realism.

I used very little black in this dress. To give it depth, I mostly used various shades of gray, along with lots of glitter pen in the bodice.

Artist's Tip

Follow the flow of the fabric with your marker strokes for a natural look.

Thin stress lines at the waist add to the texture and flow of the fabric.

The frilly bottom, drop sleeves, and fitted top make this dress perfect for hitting the dance floor.

I used three shades of green to achieve shading and lots of glitter pen on the bodice and ruffles.

The top of this dress is form-fitting, while the bottom flares out with ruffles.

Add color with your favorite markers or colored pencils, using the lightest shade to fill an area and the medium and darker shades to add curves and shading.

Workwear Ready

Note how the creases in the sleeves and body of this dress shirt make the garment fit better and look more natural.

I used two shades of lime green for the overall color and a metallic gel pen for polka dots.

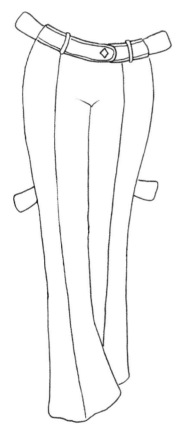

Trace the pants around your doll, keeping the legs wide at the bottom. Thin lines down the front, along with a belt and diamond-shaped button, add to the classic look.

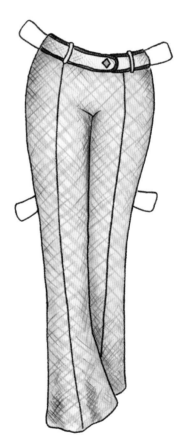

To create a plaid effect, start with a light overall color, and then add various sizes of strokes over the pants. Add a bit of shading and, as a finishing touch, use a very sharp colored pencil to add thin lines and crosshatching.

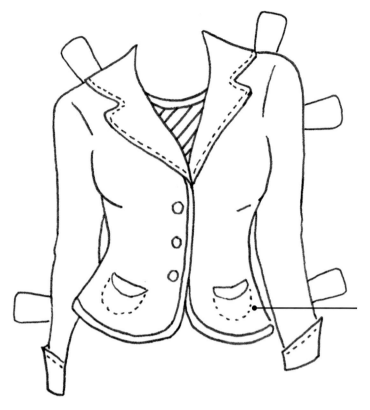

For a fitted blazer, trace your design closely around the doll. You can also add a shirt under the blazer.

Add button and pocket details and little dashes along the collar, pockets, and cuffs for topstitching.

Trace closely to the doll's figure for a fitted pencil skirt. Add flared pockets, a banded waistband, and two slits down the front for a classic style.

Add three tension lines through the middle to create movement.

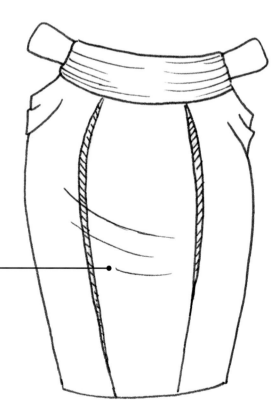

This blazer makes a bold statement with its bright red color, perfect for the office or a night out on the town.

White highlights suggest shiny leather.

Leave some white highlights, and add a few crosshatched marks with colored pencil to ramp up the texture.

I used several gray markers—plus red for the slits—to color this classic skirt.

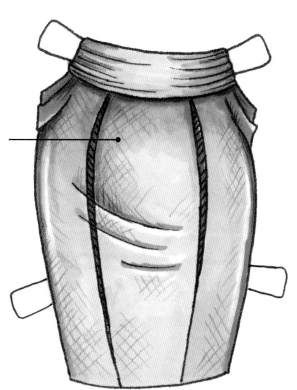

Accessories & Shoes

One of the best parts of dressing up is accessorizing! From shoes and purses to jewelry and headpieces, you can create multiple looks by mixing and matching.

Bangle Bracelet

Floral Headpiece

Purses

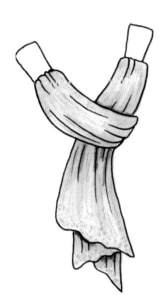

Scarf

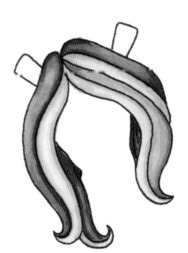

Wig

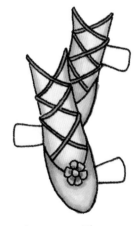

Lace-up Shoes

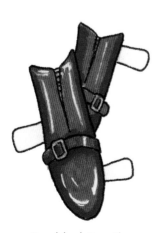

Buckled Booties

Black Boots

CHAPTER 4
Seasonal Looks

The Style Maven

No matter the season, a style maven always knows how to put together a fabulous outfit. From summery dresses to chic winter wear, she's always dressed to kill.

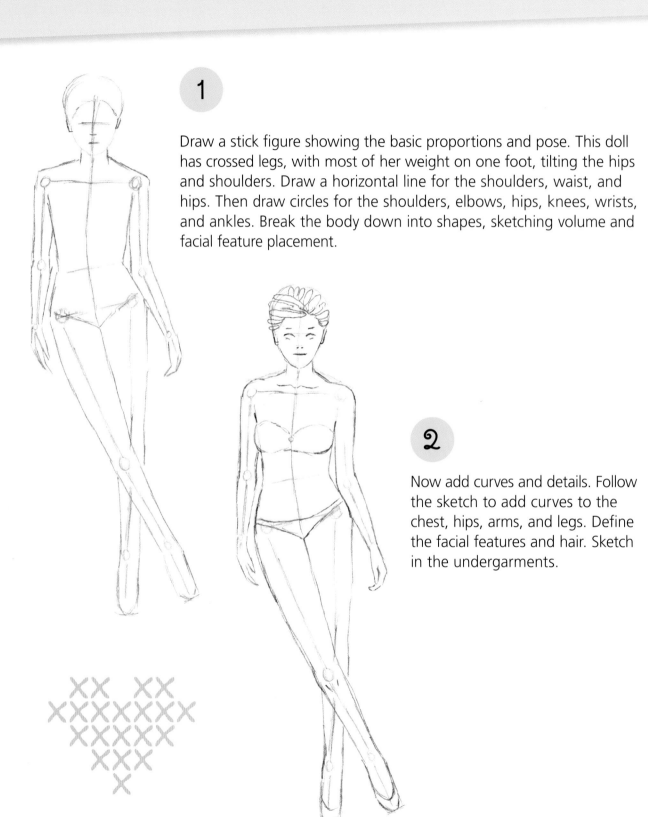

1

Draw a stick figure showing the basic proportions and pose. This doll has crossed legs, with most of her weight on one foot, tilting the hips and shoulders. Draw a horizontal line for the shoulders, waist, and hips. Then draw circles for the shoulders, elbows, hips, knees, wrists, and ankles. Break the body down into shapes, sketching volume and facial feature placement.

2

Now add curves and details. Follow the sketch to add curves to the chest, hips, arms, and legs. Define the facial features and hair. Sketch in the undergarments.

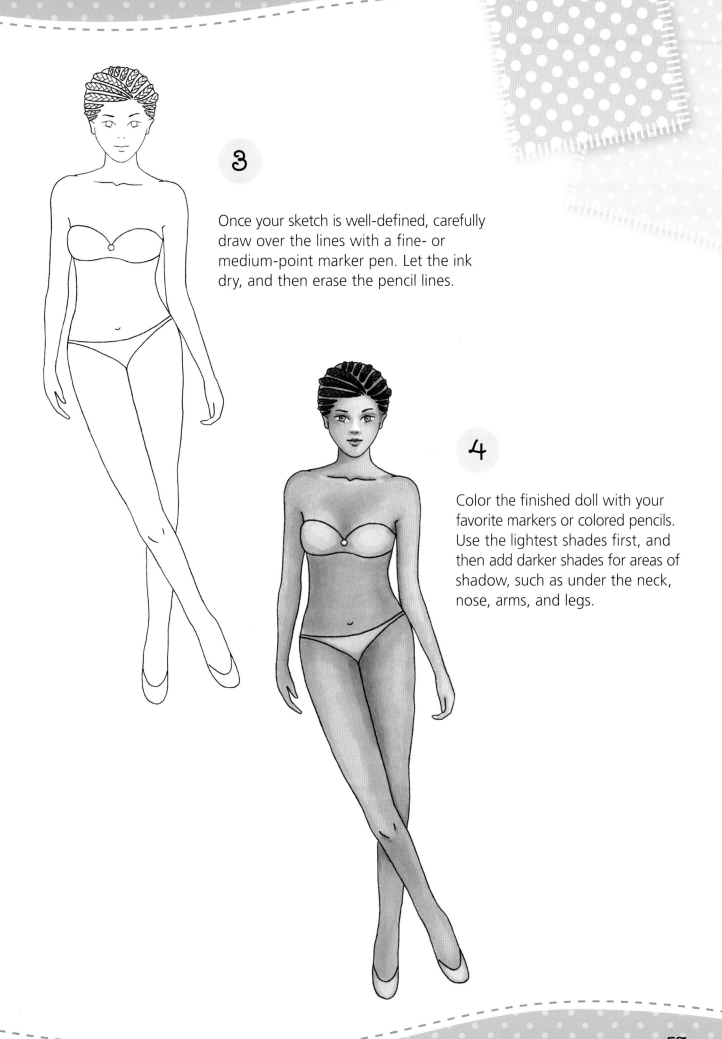

3

Once your sketch is well-defined, carefully draw over the lines with a fine- or medium-point marker pen. Let the ink dry, and then erase the pencil lines.

4

Color the finished doll with your favorite markers or colored pencils. Use the lightest shades first, and then add darker shades for areas of shadow, such as under the neck, nose, arms, and legs.

Haute Summer Sundress

When the sun is shining and the air is warm, there's nothing better than a cute sundress to bring a little style to those lazy summer days!

1

Design your dress by tracing around the doll. I added pleats, a belted waist, and a band across the top and finished with a small flower accent at the waist. I also added a flower print on the fabric.

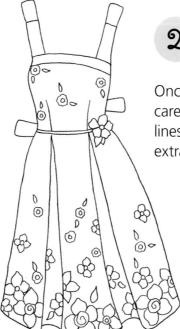

2

Once the sketch is complete, carefully draw over your pencil lines with pen, and erase any extra pencil marks.

Artist's Tip

When drawing a pattern like this in pleated areas, have some of the flowers end on the folds—this gives the illusion that the flower or pattern continues under the fold.

3

Now you're ready for color! Choose a palette that is summery and bright. I used several shades of aqua blue, with yellow and orange for the flowers. This style maven is cool and breezy...ready for a stroll on the boardwalk or a family cookout!

Fashion-forward Swimwear & Accessories

Decked out in this fashionable tankini, any style maven is ready for some fun in the sun—just don't forget the sunscreen!

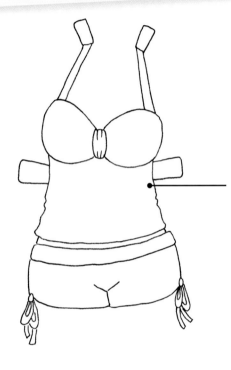

1

Design the swimsuit by tracing around the doll's body. I chose a tankini, but you can design any kind of swimsuit you like.

Design the suit as one piece, and give it the illusion of being a two-piece suit by coloring the area in between with skin tones.

Create a fun wrap for your doll, with flowing fabric that gathers on one side. Add a button and flowing ties for a loose, comfortable feel.

2

Add color. I used bright red and gray for the suit and several shades of yellow and gold on the wrap for a sunny feel. Red ties complement the swimsuit.

Trace around the doll's head to fit a floppy hat. Decorate with flowers or bows, and leave a dotted cut line where the hat will slip onto the doll's head.

I colored these shades red to match the swimsuit. Two shades of blue make the lenses look reflective.

To create a wig, trace closely around the doll's head. My doll has cornrows, so I traced over the original hair as closely as possible and then added braids down each side.

Design a colorful beach bag perfect for toting beach essentials!

Artist's Tip

When creating wigs, you want to fit the hair as closely as possible to the doll's original hair, leaving the face blank so that when you put the wig on the face shows through.

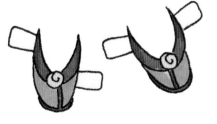

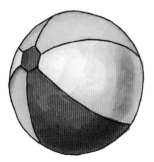

To create flip-flops, trace closely around the foot for the main shape. Add a flower and bands along the top and a line down the middle for the toes!

Autumn Cozy

In a cozy long-sleeved shirt and jeans, any trendy girl is ready for cooler temps, shorter days, and loads of fun fall activities.

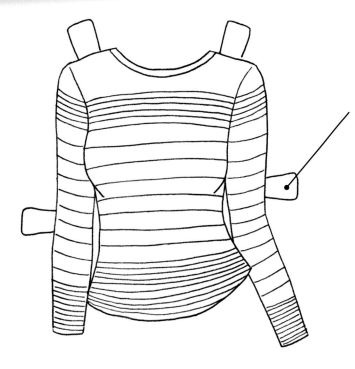

Place the tabs for long-sleeved garments on the outside of the lower arms, instead of at the waist.

To give the jeans a distressed look, add jagged squiggle areas in random spots.

Trace the t-shirt and jeans over the shape of the doll. I used a combination of wide and thin stripes for this long-sleeved tee. The jeans can be low-, mid-, or high-rise, and flared or skinny. These are the low-rise, flared jeans. To accommodate the low-rise style, I moved the tab that would normally be on the waist to the hip.

When incorporating white into your fashion designs, let the paper be white fabric, and use light or soft grays to add shading.

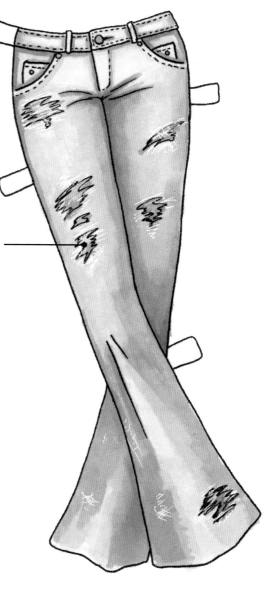

Use skin-tone shades in the distressed areas. To give the jeans an even more distressed appearance, add squiggled and hatched lines over and around the distressed areas with a white gel pen.

2

Time to add color! I used three shades of blue on the jeans to give them a worn, denim appearance. Start with the lightest blue shade, and add shading with medium and dark shades. For the shirt, I used purple and white, with orange accents for a touch of autumn color.

A tam cap adds a perfect touch of autumn cozy to any look. Trace the hat closely around the face, and add knitted texture with oval and checkerboard shapes. I used purple and fuchsia to color my tam, and a glitter pen to create a sparkly yarn effect.

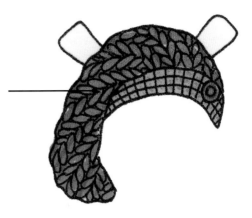

Design a classic trench coat for chillier days. Keep the outline loose and comfy when tracing around the doll. For a traditional look, use khaki and tan tones to add color, with an accent color for the trim and buttons.

A hobo bag is a must-have for all the essentials—and then some! Decorate the bag with fall leaves and add a favorite book.

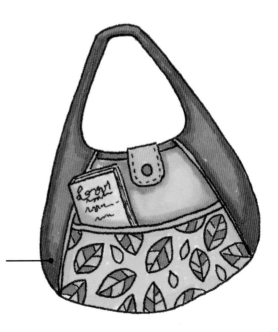

Cool and casual...ready for a day
of museum hopping and lunch
with the girls!

Winter Fabulous

Blustery days are no excuse for fashion hibernation. Use these ideas as a springboard for creating your own fabulous outfits perfect for those long winter months.

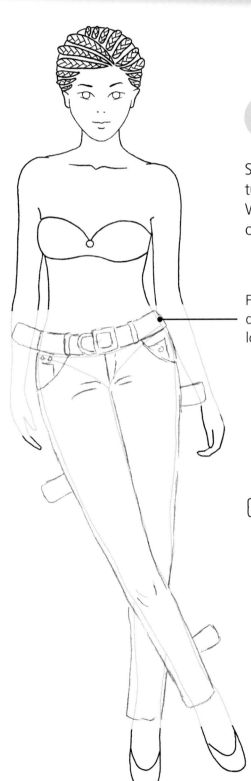

1

Sketch a pair of trendy black jeans and a cozy turtleneck to keep this stylish girl warm on chilly days. When you're happy with the sketches, trace your outlines in ink.

For skinny jeans, trace closely to the doll's shape. Add a wide belt, belt loops, pocket lines, and zipper area.

For the neck and cuffs, use simple rectangle shapes close together to give the impression of ridges. Add a belt and tabs for a classic look.

2

Add color and texture to complete your designs using colored pencils, pens, or markers.

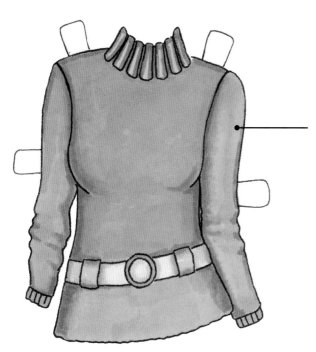

I used several shades of mint and teal greens for shading and added a gold belt for striking contrast.

I used red and black glitter gel pens for the belt and buttons to add a bit of color.

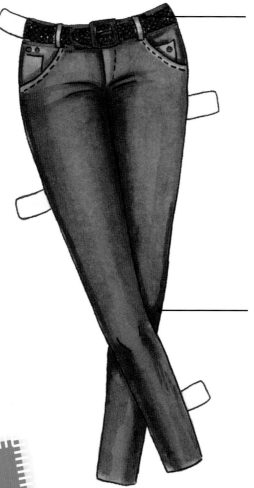

Look closely, and you'll see that there is no actual black here. I layered four different grays, as well a very dark purple, to create a dynamic black.

What better way to ward off the winter blues than with a bright gold peacoat?

To create a front-panel look, end the belt at the vertical panel line.

I used three shades of yellow for the coat and gray, black, and purple for the buttons.

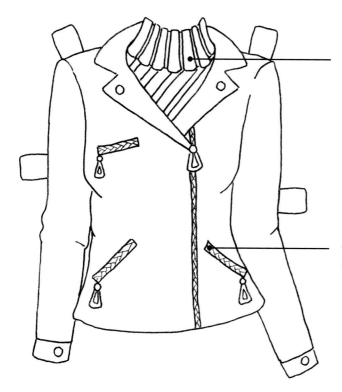

Don't forget to add a shirt beneath the jacket, such as a turtleneck.

Add details, such as zippers and buttons.

I used three shades of red to achieve shading. Be sure to leave some white highlights for shine!

I used a silver metallic gel pen for the zippers.

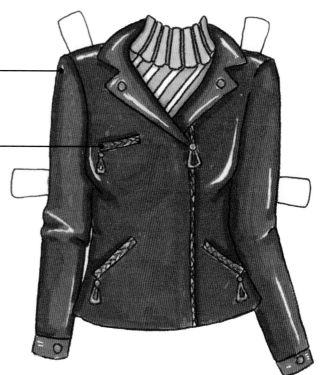

Artist's Tip

If you forget to leave the white highlights, you can add them afterward with a white gel pen.

A chic leather jacket is also the perfect finish to a fabulous winter look. You can make a classic black or tan jacket, or you can go for a fun, vibrant color like I did!

Winter is the perfect time for accessorizing. From scarves and boots to hats and gloves, the style maven can accessorize her look from head to toe!

Holiday Purse

Add loop marks throughout the scarf with a glitter gel pen to add texture and sparkle.

Infinity Scarf

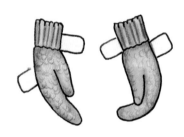

Mittens

Knit Cap

Novelty Hat

Tam Hat

Wintry Clutch

Artist's Tip

To achieve a soft plaid effect, don't draw the plaid lines with pen—use colored pencil.

Plaid Scarf

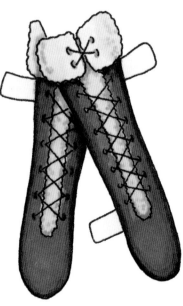

Fur-lined Boots

The combined effect is winter chic. This style maven looks stunning in gold and purple—and she's ready to face frosty weather with style and sass.

Springing Forward

Flowers in bloom, birds singing, and hints of warmer days to come...the spring season is sure to inspire new fashion ventures and colorful outfits. A feminine blouse and full skirt make the perfect outfit for embracing a season of new life.

Add a slight pucker to the top of the sleeves for a feminine look.

1

Sketch the blouse and skirt to fit the doll, following the lines and curves of the body. Once the sketch is well-defined, draw over the pencil lines with pen, and erase the pencil marks when the ink is dry.

Use a wavy line at the bottom for a ruffled effect.

2

Add color. Remember to start with the lightest colors first, and layer darker colors on top for shading.

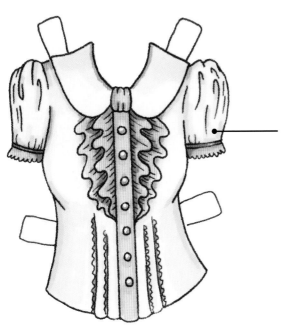

Airy spring colors, such as light lime green and soft orange, are just the right combo for this springtime top.

I used several shades of blue for the main color of the skirt, and several shades of orange for the flowers.

Backpack

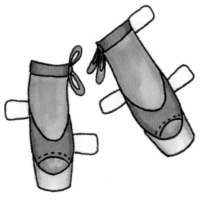

For wedge-style shoes, sketch closely to the doll's foot. Add a hole for the toes and a blocky sole on the bottom.

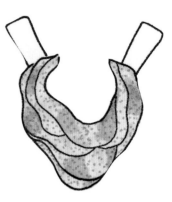

Lightweight Scarf

Colorful Patterned Scarf

Umbrella

Shoulder Bag

Purse

April showers bring May flowers—and nothing says April showers better than a bright yellow pair of rain boots.

Spring has sprung, with soft greens and bright blue skies. Dressed in a cute outfit like this, this style maven is ready to step out in style!

CHAPTER 5
Fashionable Eras

The Vogue Fashionista

Fashion has had many faces over the decades, and each one is special and unique in its own way. The vogue fashionista embraces the unique traits of each era and knows how to rock the look—no matter how many decades have passed.

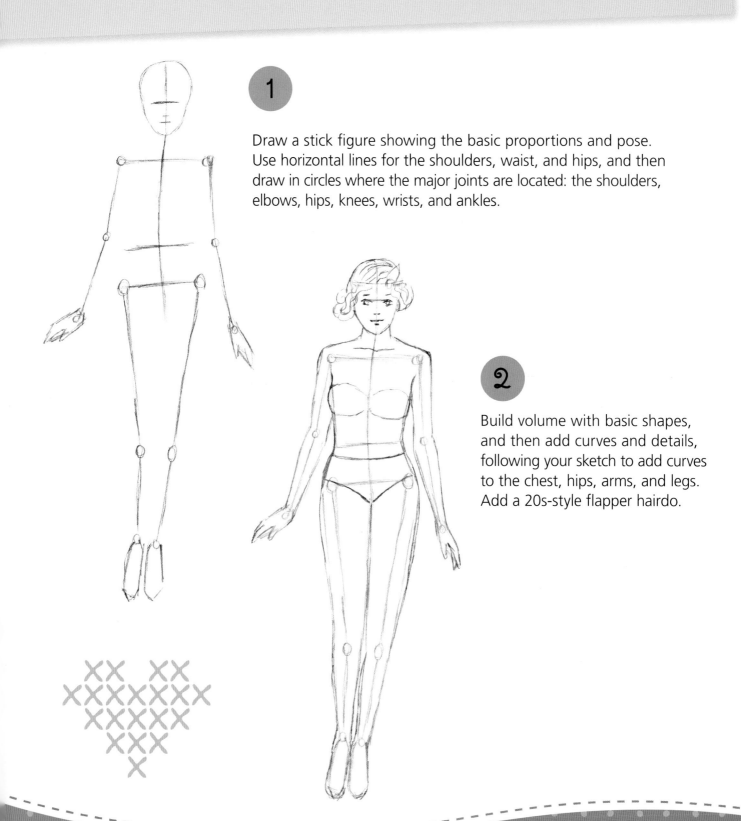

1

Draw a stick figure showing the basic proportions and pose. Use horizontal lines for the shoulders, waist, and hips, and then draw in circles where the major joints are located: the shoulders, elbows, hips, knees, wrists, and ankles.

2

Build volume with basic shapes, and then add curves and details, following your sketch to add curves to the chest, hips, arms, and legs. Add a 20s-style flapper hairdo.

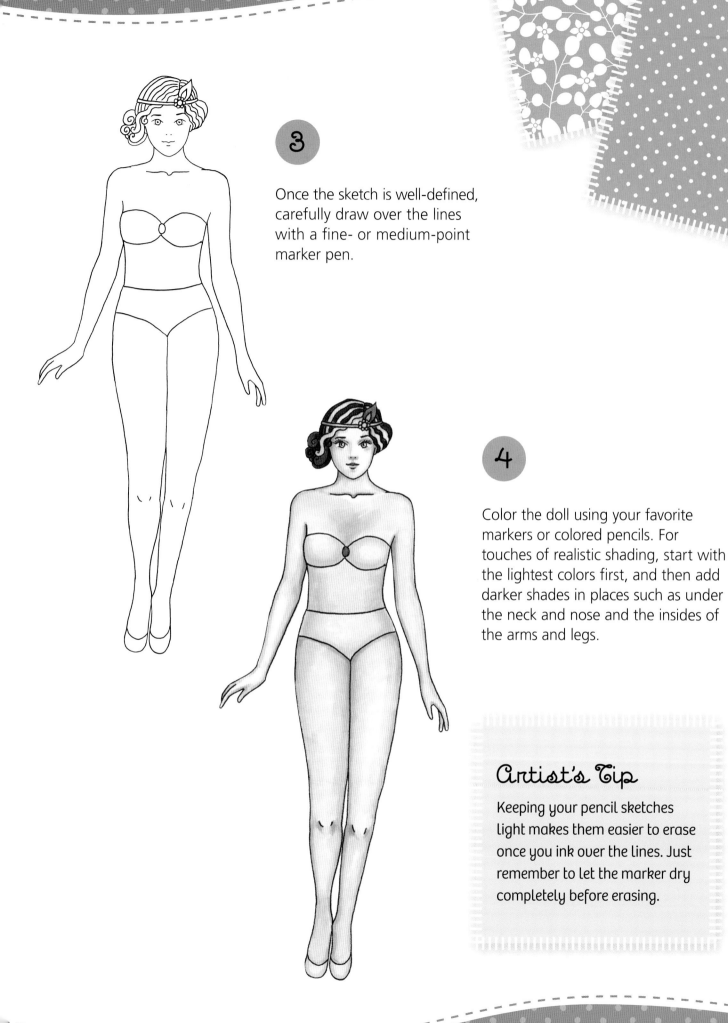

3

Once the sketch is well-defined, carefully draw over the lines with a fine- or medium-point marker pen.

4

Color the doll using your favorite markers or colored pencils. For touches of realistic shading, start with the lightest colors first, and then add darker shades in places such as under the neck and nose and the insides of the arms and legs.

Artist's Tip

Keeping your pencil sketches light makes them easier to erase once you ink over the lines. Just remember to let the marker dry completely before erasing.

The 1920s

The roaring 1920s is the decade in which fashion entered the modern era. Shapely curves were concealed, and straight lines were in. Want to dress your vogue fashionista in 1920s best? What could be better than a sassy flapper dress?

1

Draw the flapper dress by tracing around the doll.

Artist's Tip

There's no need to add all the fringe in pencil—just draw an outline where the fringe will be. This will keep your erasing to a minimum and make your drawing cleaner. Do the same for the pearls, by lightly placing a line as a guide.

2

Once the sketch is well-defined, draw over the pencil lines with pen, adding fringe to the bottom with squiggly lines and defining the pearls with small circles. Erase the pencil lines when the ink is dry.

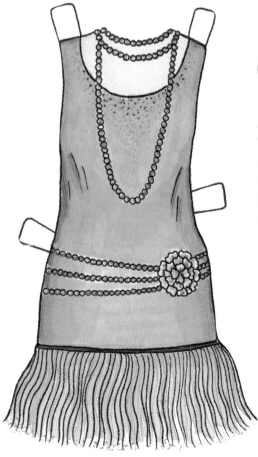

3

Add color. I layered several pinks for the base and then added shading with a darker fuchsia pink. Beading was big in the 20s, so I added "beads" on the neckline with glitter gel pens.

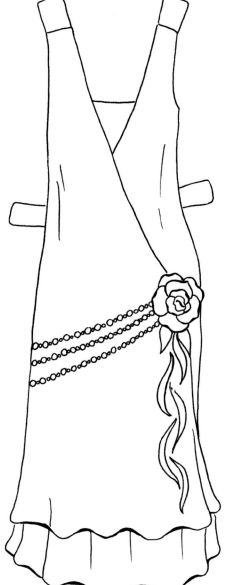

1920s clothing was glamorous, and the women were elegant. This sophisticated gown is perfect for a dinner party.

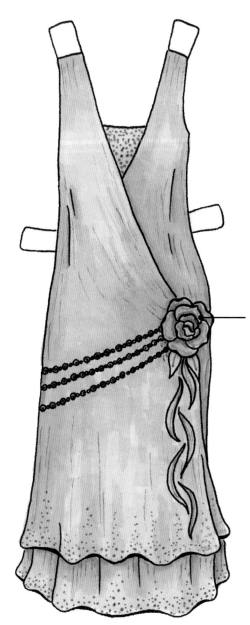

Drop waists and flowing fabrics embellished with beads and flowers are perfect for a formal dinner.

Women dressed for all occasions in the 1920s. There were riding clothes, dinner clothes—even the proper clothing to go out shopping for more outfits!

This patterned red dress fits the bill for an afternoon shopping spree!

I used a white gel pen to add the swirly pattern.

Bobbed Hat

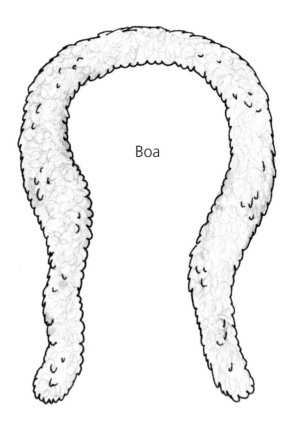

Boa

Cloche

String of Pearls

Flapper Purse

Evening Purse

Purses in the 1920s were embellished to match the beautiful dresses of the time. They were small and carried only a few items, such as makeup and money, and were considered a fashion accessory.

T-bar shoes were the most popular style of women's footwear in the 1920s.

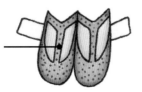

T-bar Shoes

This 1920s gal is ready for a night of jazz music, dancing, and memory-making with friends!

The 1940s

The 1940s found fashionable ladies embracing a chic yet sensible style in bright color palettes.

In the 1940s day dresses, often called shirtwaist dresses, were the most popular style of the time. It's a classic style that is still common today.

The 1940s saw women entering the workforce in large numbers, and workwear became an everyday part of a woman's wardrobe.

Evening wear in the 1940s was glamorous and often embellished with sequins and beads. Princess ball gowns embraced fitted bodices and full skirts.

Hats

Gloves

Gloves of all lengths were worn for different occasions—wrist gloves for day and long gloves for evening. White gloves are classic, but also you can also match colors to outfits for an inspired vintage look.

Purse

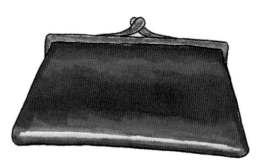

Clutch

Dress Shoes

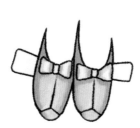

Loafers

Design a 1940s-style wig for your doll!

Sweet and chic, this 1940s icon is decked out in casual wear for a weekend outing.

The 1960s

Fashion in the 1960s was known for its bright, colorful patterns. Mix and match bold colors and incorporate geometric shapes into your designs for mod style.

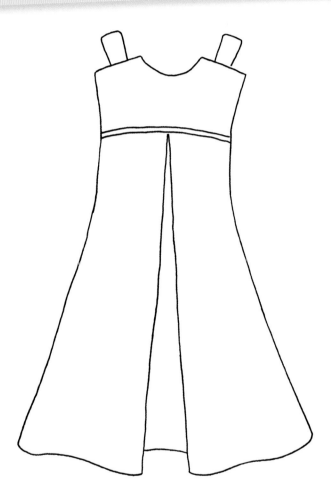

Mod dresses of the 1960s utilized bold colors and straight, shapeless profiles with short hemlines.

Introduced in the mid-1960s, go-go boots were low-heeled fashion boots named after the dance style. The slang term "go" referred to something that was all the rage.

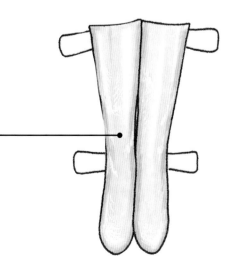

The shift or sheath dress of the 1960s came in a full rainbow of solid, bright colors, often with colorblock patterns, prints, and artistic designs.

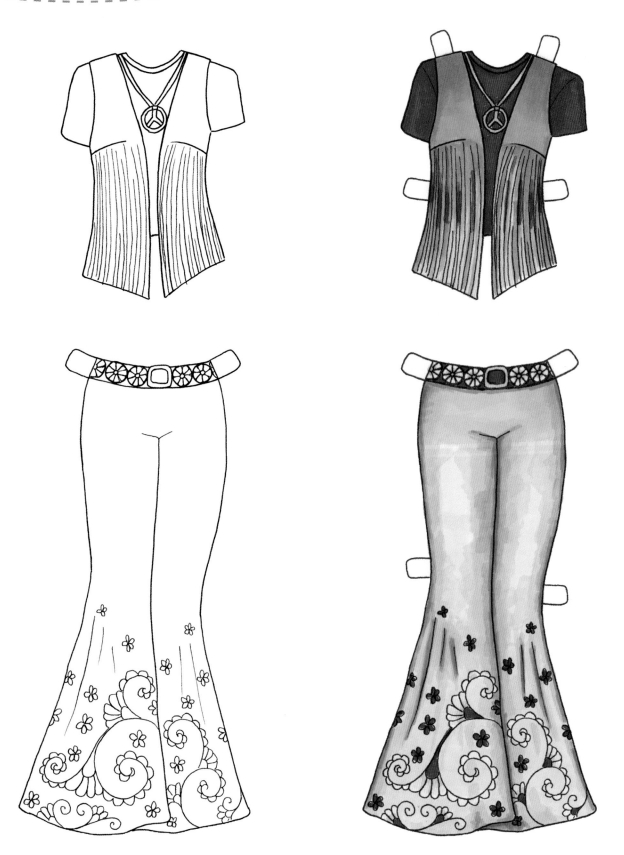

Bell-bottoms became fashionable for both men and women in the mid-1960s. These stylish bottoms flared out from the calf, had curved hems at the bottom, and were often made of denim.

Pillbox hats, named after the hexagonal cases that pills used to be sold in, were small hats with flat crowns and straight, upright sides.

A shift mini dress paired with go-go boots is the perfect look for this cool gal!

Black patent leather was in. White highlights emphasize the shiny look.

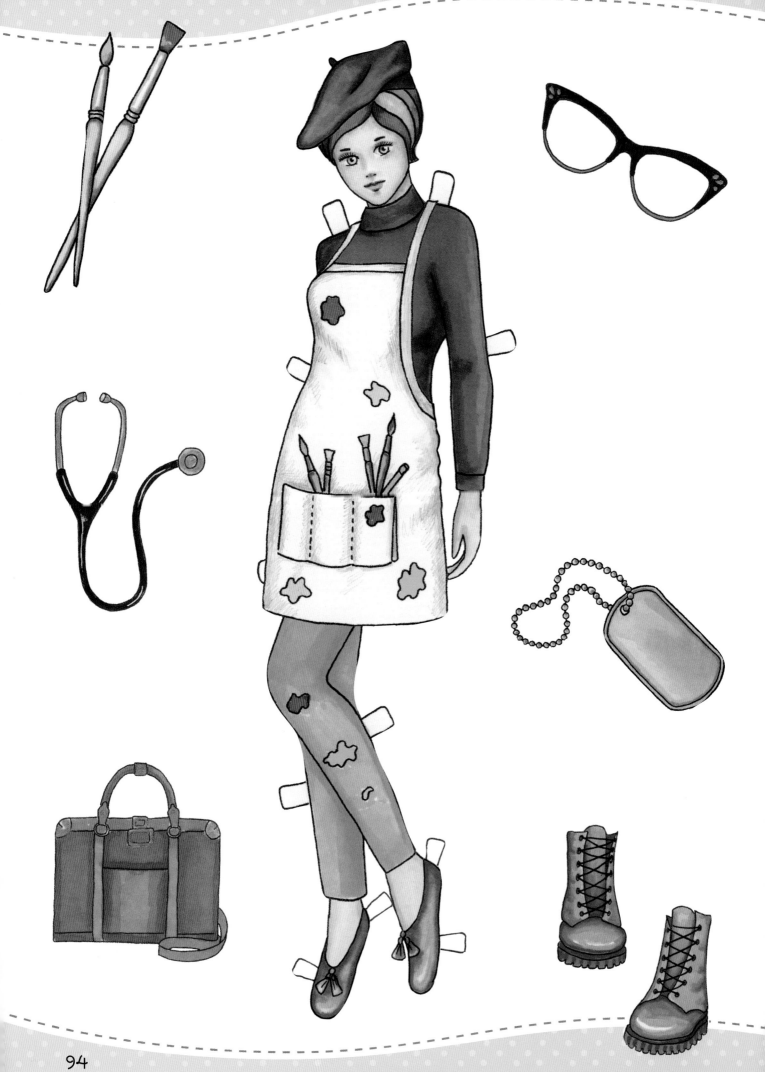

CHAPTER 6

Careers

Doctor

She loves to take care of others, she works well under pressure, and she knows how to make important decisions. You can easily change this look up by creating a pair of scrubs for a nurse, or even a surgeon's outfit!

Sketch the doctor's outfit over the doll. Instead of making a separate top, bottom, and lab coat, I created one solid outfit, creating the illusion of a shirt and skirt under the coat.

Serviceperson

This dedicated member of the Armed Services is loyal, resilient, and competent.

Sketch the fatigues outfit over the doll. Instead of making a separate top, bottom, and boots, it's easier to create one solid outfit, giving the illusion of separate pieces.

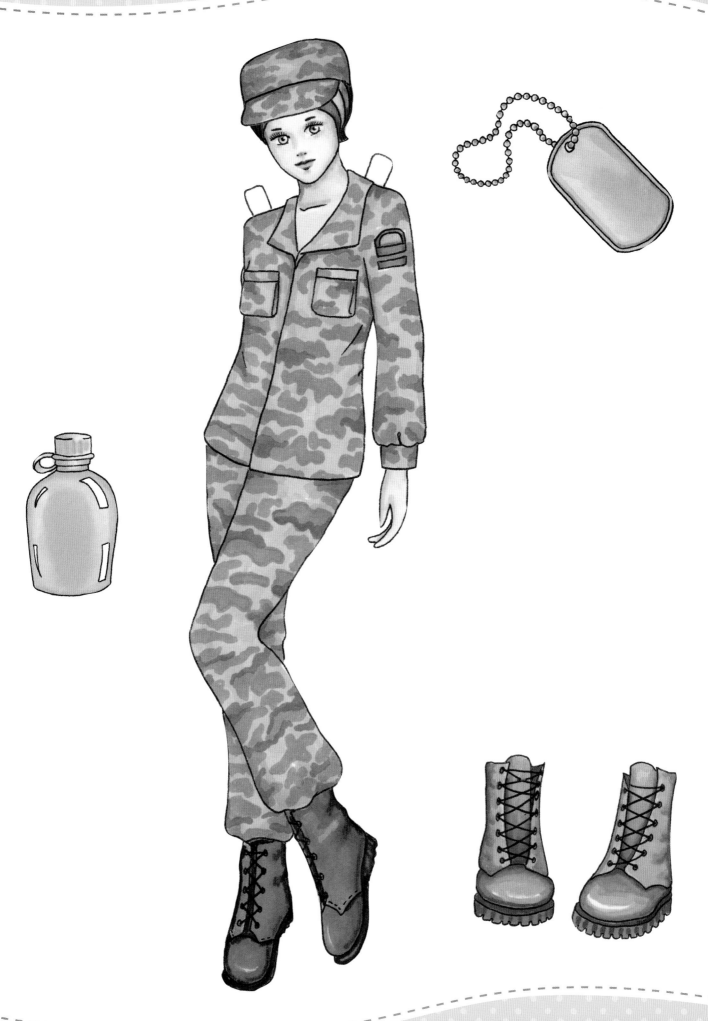

Executive

This high-powered executive has style, class, and moxie. She's chic and sophisticated, but she also knows how to have fun.

Sketch the skirt, blazer, and shirt collar over the doll. Choose a neutral shade for the suit or a gorgeous jewel tone, like this blue!

Artist

This free-spirited artist loves to create. Her days are filled with paint, palettes, and soon-to-be-masterpieces!

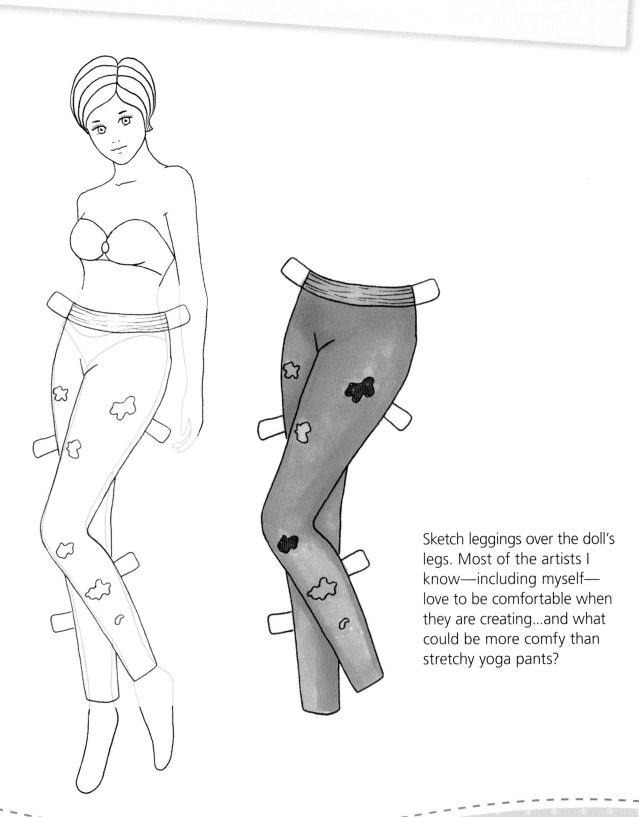

Sketch leggings over the doll's legs. Most of the artists I know—including myself—love to be comfortable when they are creating...and what could be more comfy than stretchy yoga pants?

Sketch the turtleneck over the doll's torso.

Sketch an apron over the doll.
Be sure to take into consideration
that it needs to fit over both
the clothing and the doll—you
may want to make the tabs a
bit longer.

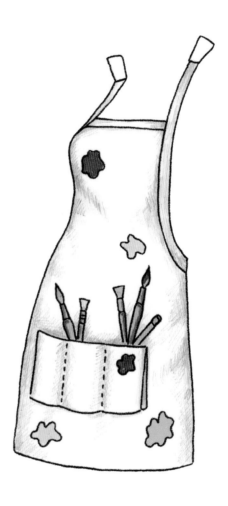

CHAPTER 7
Costume & Couture

The Visionary Fashion Mogul

From the runway to a costume party to a joyful walk down the chapel aisle, inspiration abounds for the visionary fashion mogul.

1

Draw a stick figure showing the basic proportions and pose. This doll has a slight tilt to the head and body, so I used a curved center line. Draw horizontal lines for the shoulders, waist, and hips, and then draw in circles where the major joints are located. Then break down the body into basic shapes, and draw diagonal lines connecting the waist to the shoulders and hips. Sketch in volume in the arms and legs.

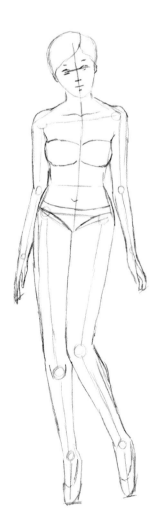

2

Now add curves and details. Follow the sketch to add curves to the chest, hips, arms, and legs. Sketch in horizontal lines for the facial feature placement, and add some hair.

Artist's Tip

Keep your pencil sketches light so that they are easier to erase. My sketches are darker than normal for demonstration purposes.

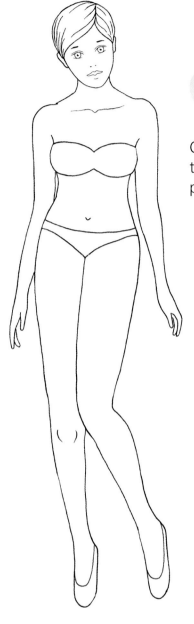

Once the sketch is well-defined, carefully trace over the lines with a fine- or medium-point marker pen.

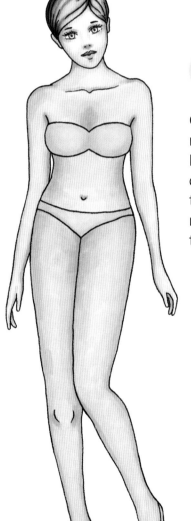

4

Color the doll using your favorite markers or colored pencils. Remember to start with the lightest colors first for a base of color, and then add darker shades under the neck and nose and the insides of the arms and legs.

Bridal

There are so many elegant and stylish styles of wedding dresses! This A-line look features a romantic sweetheart neckline, empire waist, and layers of sparkly fabric.

1

Draw the wedding dress by tracing around the doll. To achieve the illusion of a sleeveless gown, draw the area between the shoulders and top of the bodice and color it with matching skin tones. Place the tabs in their usual spot on the tops of the shoulders. This also is a great way to add a necklace! Once the sketch is well-defined, draw over the pencil lines with pen, and erase the pencil.

Be sure to trim away the black outlines here for that perfect illusion neckline when you dress your doll.

2

Add color. I used a light silver gray and left mostly white paper showing through. I used a peach accent for the flower and added fringed lace to the dress layers. I also used a silver glitter pen and a clear star glitter pen to add sparkle along the edge of each layer.

For an elegant mermaid wedding dress or gown, trace the top closely to the doll's figure, with a wide, flared bottom with ruffled fabric on both sides.

Add sequins and rhinestones on one side of the dress and a ruffle at the top of the sleeve.

I used creams and silver-blues to give this wedding dress a touch of color. I also added little dots of blue sparkle gel pen for shimmer and shine.

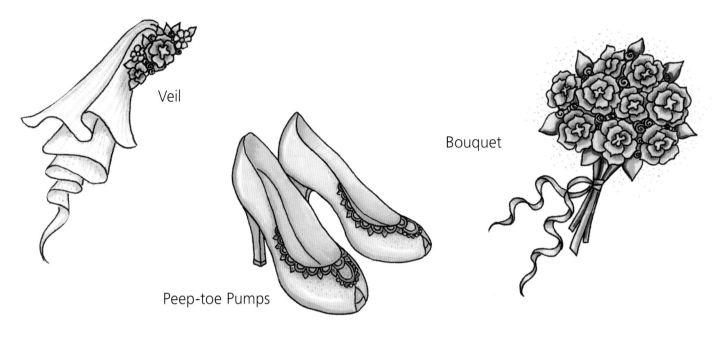

Veil

Peep-toe Pumps

Bouquet

Garter

Bridal Clutch

Bridal Updo

Trace the hairstyle over the doll's head, making sure to cover the existing hair.

Finalize the lines with pen.

Add color. This blonde hair nicely offsets the silver headpiece.

All dressed up and ready to say,
"I do," in beautiful style.

Victorian

Ruffles, lace, roses, pulled-in waistlines, and full skirts are classic details of the Victorian era.

1

Trace the dress over the doll's figure. Make the skirt nice and full, which accentuates the waist. Ink over the pencil when you're happy with the look, and erase the pencil marks.

Add color! I chose an exciting and vibrant color palette for this fun dress. Note how the complementary blue and orange colors help make the dress "pop."

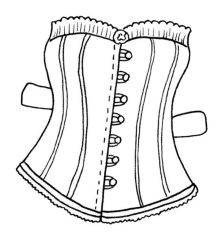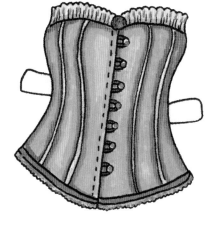

Corset

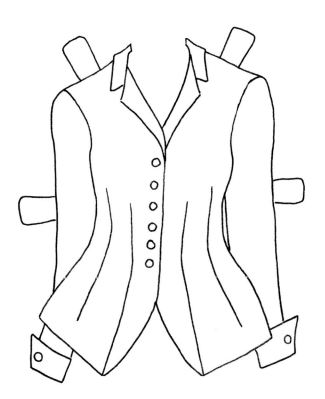

Riding Jacket

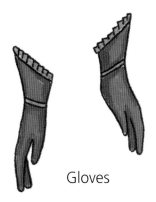

Gloves

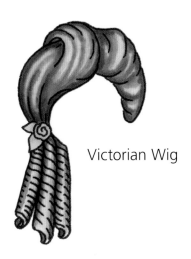

Victorian Wig

Fan

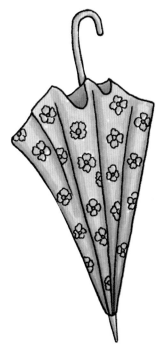

Parasol

Victorian Shoes

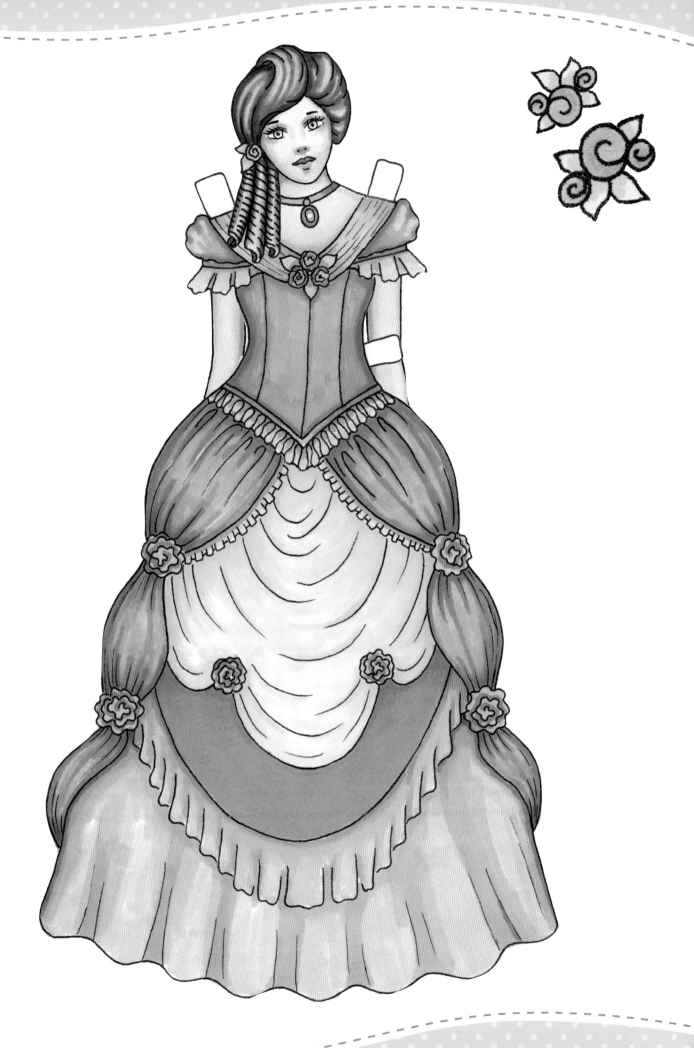

Renaissance

Renaissance fashion was marked by contrasting fabrics, embroidery, trims, and other forms of surface ornamentation.

1

Start with the outline of the dress, as usual. Add decorative trim at the ends of the billowy sleeves, the waist, the neckline, and the opening of the dress overlay.

2

Add color. Clothing in this era was relatively simple, without a great deal of ornamentation or embellishment.

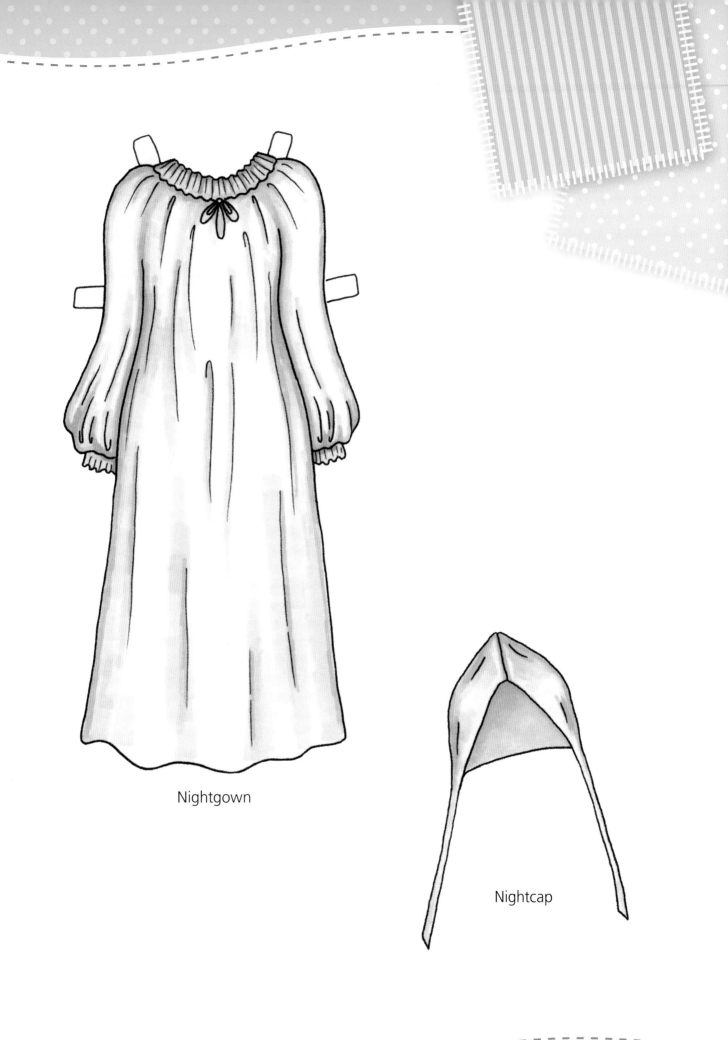

Nightgown

Nightcap

Renaissance Wig

Brooch

Mask

Neck Ruff

Renaissance Shoes

Runway Ready

When it comes to runway fashion, there are no limits. You can design something funky and bold or ethereal and dreamy—or anything in between!

1

Trace this runway-fabulous dress over the doll's body. To create the look of tulle in the underskirt, use simple squiggle lines.

2

Nothing is more dramatic than red!
You don't need to do anything to
the tulle underskirt, other than lay
down light color.

Make the perfect pair of
shiny red pumps to match!

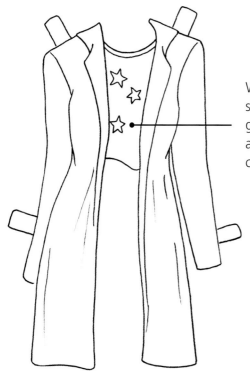

When designing an open shirt or jacket, draw the garment underneath as part of the piece of clothing.

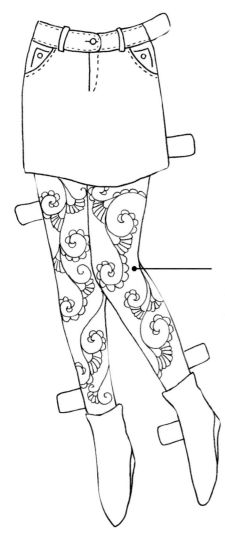

Instead of drawing a separate skirt, leggings, and boots, I combined all three into one illustration. You can design clothing this way or as separate pieces— whichever way you choose is fine!

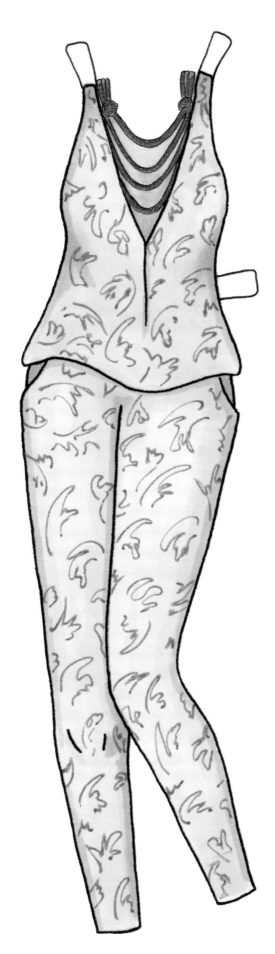

Create a fun and edgy romper by drawing an invisible neckline and layered necklace.

Fun and casual!

Ready to rock the runway!

About the Artist

Norma J. Burnell, Certified Zentangle® Teacher, is an accomplished artist and has been involved in the arts all of her life. She is the illustrator for two adult coloring books, **Messages from The Fairies** (2016) and **Messages from Your Angels** (2016) and is a contributing author to **The Art of Zentangle**® (2013) and to **The Art of Fashion Tangling** (2016).

After discovering the art of Zentangle®, Norma began incorporating "tangles" into her own fantasy art and "Fairy-Tangles™" was born. Many of her Fairy-Tangles™ drawings have been converted to rubber stamp designs for cardmaking and other crafts, and her originals have been sold to collectors around the world.

Norma currently works for a small company creating websites and graphic designs. She also teaches various art classes and continues to develop her own art. Her lifelong dream is to continue being an artist and to share her art with others. She resided in the seaside community of Jamestown with her husband and three-legged cat, Ruckus, who lives up to his name.

Find out more at www.fairy-tangles.com.

USING THE PAPER DOLL MODELS

On the following pages, you'll find four model cutouts to jumpstart your paper doll fashion journey. Tear out the pages, and carefully cut out the dolls along the dotted lines. Then use the dolls to trace and design your own paper doll wardrobe. Use these models as a starting point, and refer to the tips and instructions on pages 16-18 to create additional paper dolls in a variety of poses!

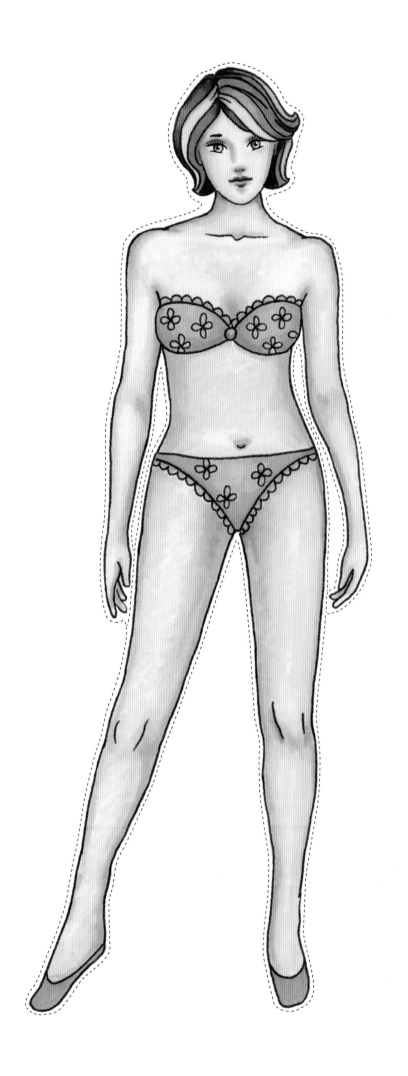

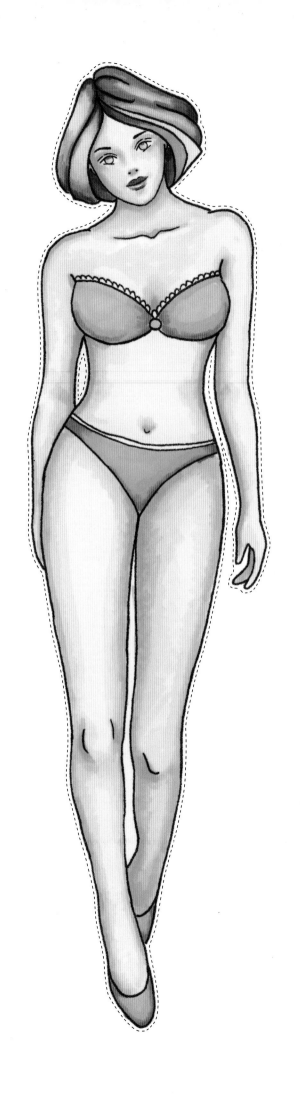

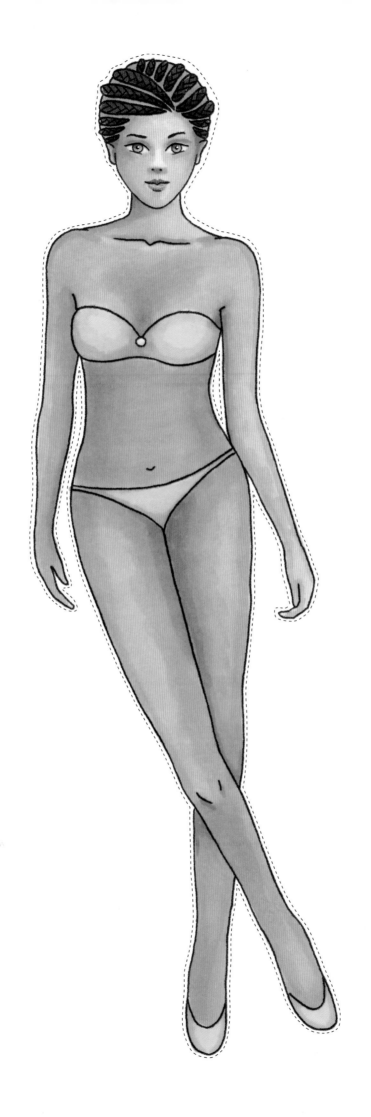

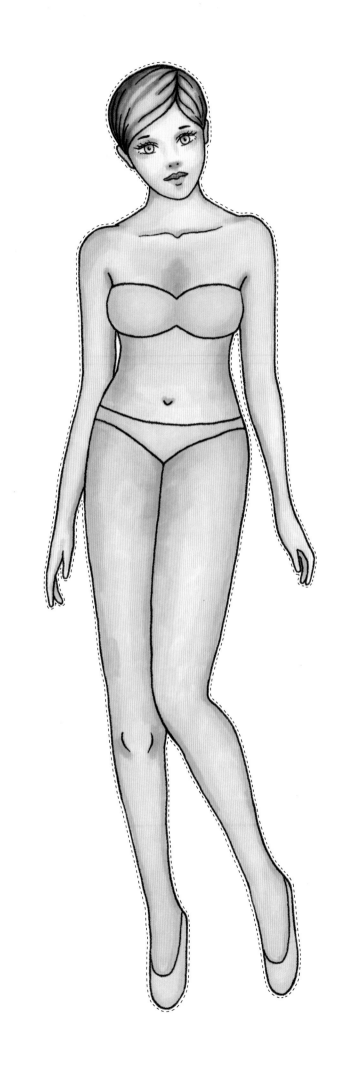